TRUMP

The
Puzzle Book

For
very
Stable
GeNiuSeS

Published by and Copyright © Secret Santa Seasonal Stuff
SecretSantaSeasonalStuff@gmail.com

Looking for bespoke novelty publications? Contact us for a quote.

This product is for amusement only, and any similarity to the real Donald Trump is purely coincidental. We're sure he can't be as bad as the Mainstream Media say he is. Can he?

INStruCtioNS

Use your knowledge of that modern wonder of the world (Donald Trump) to solve the puzzles contained within.

Good luck.

Complete the Quote

The four words below have been anagrammed. Can you rearrange the letters and place the resulting words in the spaces to complete the Trump quote?

IFTFH

VANEEU

HSOOT

OVETSR

"I could stand in the middle of

_____ _____

and _____ somebody

and I wouldn't lose _____."

6

"Why are we having all these people from **shit** *hole* *countries come here?"*

SHiTHoLe COUNtrieS

How familiar are you with the 'shithole' countries in Africa? You know, the type of place where Trump has said his friends go to get rich at someone else's expense. Using Trumpian logic, and the clues below, identify the countries.

1. Trump refers to this country as 'Nambia'.

2. "I really like Nelson Mandela but _____ is a crime ridden mess that is just waiting to explode – not a good situation for the people!"

3. Trump placed a random travel ban on this country – one apparent reason for this ban being that the country ran out of passport paper.

4. This country retaliated to Trump's 'shithole countries' remark with '#mywaterhole'.

5. Trump spells this country as 'Somolia'.

TWeet TeSt

Take thirty seconds to memorize these snippets
from Trump's tweets. When you're finished,
turn to the next page and test your memory.

TWeet TeSt

Write each snippet back in its original speech bubble, then check back to the previous page to see how you did.

"Many are saying I'm the best 140 character writer in the world. It's easy when it's fun."

"In addition to winning the Electoral College in a landslide, I won the popular vote if you deduct the millions of people who voted illegally."

RebUS RiddLe

Try to identify the idiom that Trump used in a tweet about Russia, as clued by the following:

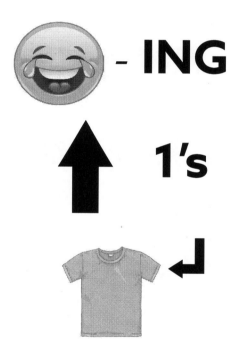

"Why would Kim Jong-un insult me by calling me 'old' when I would NEVER call him 'short and fat?' Oh well, I try so hard to be his friend – and maybe someday that will happen."

MuddLed-up Besties

Unscramble the words below to reveal the people that Trump enjoys engaging in quality conversations with.

For example, 'Dump Old Rant' could be unscrambled to read 'Donald Trump'.

I NEED JOB

AM A BACK BOAR

MUN JOKING

DUMP RIVAL IN IT

"*I'm intelligent. Some people would say
I'm very, very, very intelligent.*"

Veiled Verse

Find one of Trump's preferred words (which are of course in no way a reflection of his character) hidden in each line of the poem below.

For example: Wo**man, I ac**tually cannot
believe you expect respect! (**Maniac**)

He is not merely a gigolo serenading citizens for votes – he is
Donald Trump (5)

He will bust up ideals that he doesn't agree with (6)

And heroize roaches who are morally facetious (4)

Despite his guru decorum (4)

And his believable spun fairy tales (5)

His ethic lowness will always prevail (5)

"It's really cold outside, they are calling it a major freeze, weeks ahead of normal. Man, we could use a big fat dose of global warming!"

19

Global WARNING

A simple test of your climate-change knowledge.

Why did Trump decide to pull the USA out of the Paris Agreement?

1. It's so cold in New York, they need global warming.

2. Climate change is a hoax.

3. It would have cost the USA trillions of dollars.

4. It is possible he is a huge buffoon.

5. All of the above.

*"I will be phenomenal to the women.
I mean, I want to help women."*

Zigzag

Complete the zigzag by using the last two letters of the preceding word as the first two letters of the next word.

Please note that these words are not in any way allusions to Trump's character.

| P | R | E | D | A | T | | |

"I will build a great wall – and nobody builds walls better than me, believe me – and I'll build them very inexpensively. I will build a great, great wall on our southern border, and I will make Mexico pay for that wall. Mark my words."

THe WaLL

Help Trump build his wall, even if you aren't Mexican. He needs all the help he can get.

The wall needs to join all of the posts together so that every post is used by two wall panels. The resulting wall must form a single loop that creates one single area inside the wall – all the better for keeping the immigrants out. Wall panels can only be placed horizontally or vertically.

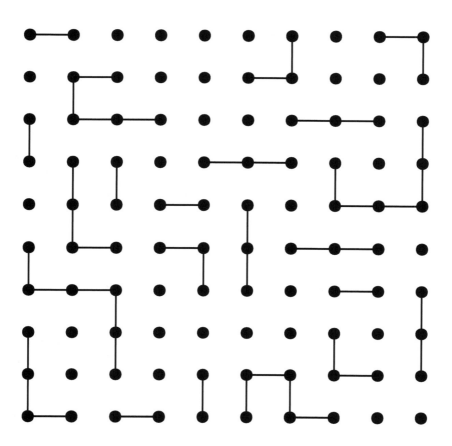

Making Sense of Trump

Trump's words are such a pleasure to read. It would be a gross injustice if one were to misunderstand them.

Decode this Trump quote by cracking the Caesar cipher. Shift each letter a consistent amount forwards or backwards through the alphabet. For example, you might replace A with C, B with D and so on until you replace Y with A and Z with B.

O'BK YGOJ OL OBGTQG CKXKT'Z SE JGAMNZKX, VKXNGVY O'J HK JGZOTM NKX.

"*Well, if I ever ran for office, I'd do better as a Democrat than as a Republican - and that's not because I'd be more liberal, because I'm conservative. But the working guy would elect me. He likes me. When I walk down the street, those cabbies start yelling out their windows.*"

Dot-to-Dot Drawing

"Will someone from [Kim Jong-un's] regime please inform him that I too have a nuclear button, but it is a much bigger and powerful one than his, and my button works!"

Weird Wording

Can you rewrite each of the following
to reveal a Trump trope?

For example: 'A great quantity of currency'
can be re-expressed as 'a lot of money'.

Not good hairstyles with tones of dyes that shade into each other.

Not losing one more time.

"Certain guys tell me they want women of substance, not beautiful models. It just means they can't get beautiful models."

Word PyraMid

Complete the word pyramid using the clues provided.

Each clue below corresponds to a level of the pyramid, which indicates the length of the word. Each level of the pyramid uses the same letters as the level above but with one letter added on each row. The letters can be rearranged in each row.

1. **Not good**. As in, "Trump is a *not good* president."

2. **Pats**. As in, "my granny *pats* her teary eyes every time she hears Trump speak."

3. **Founded**. As in, "Trump's presidency is *founded* on lunacy."

4. **Prejudiced**. As in, "Trump's policies are *prejudiced*."

5. **Deactivate**. As in, "someone *deactivate* Trump's Twitter."

6. **Degrading**. As in, "when Trump refers to Mexican immigrants as rapists and criminals, he is obviously *degrading* them."

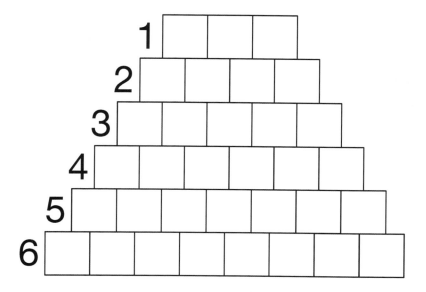

"Any negative polls are fake news"

Climate Conundrum

Okay, the joke is over. In case you're wondering who the real perpetrators are, give this logic puzzle a go.

Using the information below, figure out the percentage of CO_2 emissions of each country mentioned and the action that each country has taken against climate change.

- The four countries with the highest CO_2 emissions in the world are the USA, China, India and Russia.

- The percentages CO_2 emissions of these countries are 28%, 15%, 6% and 5%.

- Steps are being taken by each country to deal with this. Namely: capping coal consumption; supporting the Paris Agreement; fighting air pollution; and leaving the Paris agreement.

- The USA's emissions are higher than India's, which is not the lowest.

- The country that left the Paris Agreement is the second highest CO_2 contributor.

- The country who supports the agreement is the lowest CO_2 contributor.

- The country with 28% emissions will cap coal consumption.

- The country with the highest emissions is earliest in the alphabet.

"Show me someone with no ego and I'll

show you a ***big loser"***

Missing Link

Each of the following pairs of words secretly conceals a third word. This third word can be added to the end of the first word, and the start of the second word, to form two new words. Can you reveal all four hidden words?

For example: PUT_____ DANCE could be solved by **RID** to make PUT**RID** and **RID**DANCE

NON _____ **LESS**

DIS _____ **HEM**

BULL _____ **TING**

OVER _____ **SOME**

"My fingers are long and beautiful, as, it has been well documented, are various other parts of my body."

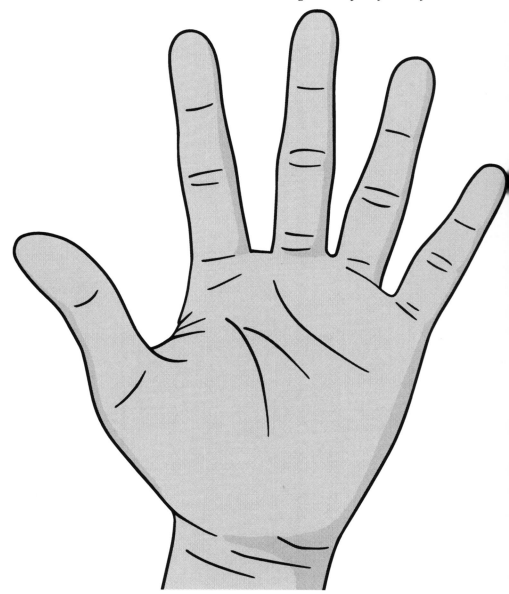

RebuS RiddLe

Can you identify this phrase that is
regularly used by Trump?

OF

"*The media – really, the word, I think one of the greatest of all terms I've come up with – is*

fake."

I'M Trumped

Choose a word or phrase of your choice from the right-hand column to complete each numbered sentence.

1. Hold my _____.

2. Ivanka Trump is _____ in Trump's agenda.

3. _____ were walking down the road.

4. We must do _____ better.

5. This is a _____ win.

6. They're not false, but rather _____.

7. Be sure to find a _____ to deal with your legal matter.

"Council"

"Yuge"

"Covfefe"

"Alternative Facts"

"Two Corinthians"

"Cyber"

"Complicit"

Reporter: How are you going to build a 1,900-mile wall?

Trump: Very easy. I'm a builder. That's easy. I build buildings that are — can I tell you what's more complicated? What's more complicated is building a building that's 95 stories tall. OK?

WaLLed IN

Uh oh. It looks like Trump couldn't afford the best architects and isn't quite the builder he thinks he is. The wall has been built around him!

Can you help Trump get out? (Assuming you want to)

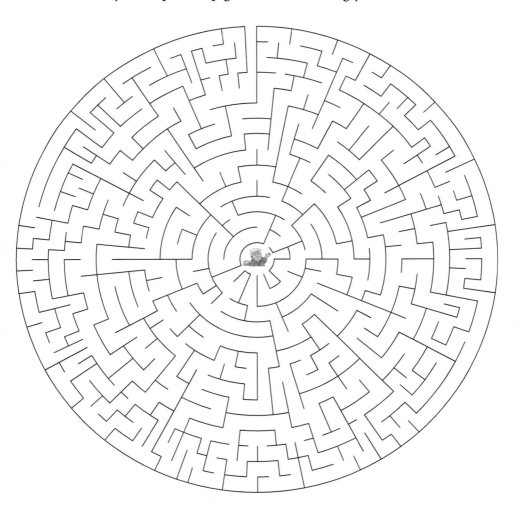

*"I say, not in a braggadocios way, I've made
billions and billions of dollars dealing
with people all around the world."*

Making Sense of Trump

Trump's words are such a pleasure to read that it would be a gross injustice if one were to misunderstand them. Even so, sometimes they need to be concealed to protect the innocent.

Lose your innocence by decoding this Trump quote. Simply shift each letter a constant amount forwards or backwards through the alphabet. For example, you might replace A with C, B with D and so on until you replace Y with A and Z with B.

L'P WKH OHDVW UDFLVW SHUVRQ BRX KDYH HYHU LQWHUYLHZHG

"As a kid, I was making a building with blocks in our playroom. I didn't have enough. So I asked my younger brother Robert if I could borrow some of his. He said, 'Okay, but you have to give them back when you're done.' I used all of my blocks, then all of his blocks, and when I was done I had a great building, which I then glued together.

Robert never did get those blocks back."

"Word" Search

Try to find the word 'covfefe', as featured
in those immortal Trumpian words:
"Despite the constant negative press COVFEFE."

V	V	E	O	O	V	O	V	E	C	E	E	E	F	V
F	F	E	C	C	F	V	O	E	E	E	O	C	F	V
F	E	O	C	F	E	V	E	F	O	F	F	V	F	O
C	E	F	F	E	V	O	O	E	E	F	O	V	C	C
E	V	O	E	E	E	C	F	E	F	C	O	C	E	E
C	F	E	O	F	V	O	F	E	F	E	E	E	O	E
O	O	C	C	F	E	E	F	E	F	E	F	F	F	O
E	V	E	V	V	V	E	F	F	E	E	E	E	F	C
O	F	F	O	E	F	E	F	E	O	C	F	F	E	F
F	E	O	F	C	C	E	V	V	E	O	O	V	C	F
V	V	O	O	O	E	E	F	E	F	F	C	C	O	F
E	F	O	V	E	O	E	F	E	V	F	V	F	V	C
O	O	F	F	F	E	F	C	F	F	F	C	E	O	O
E	V	F	O	V	E	E	F	E	E	F	V	F	V	F
F	V	V	E	C	C	E	C	F	E	F	V	E	O	E

"Nobody has better respect for intelligence than Donald Trump"

Word PyraMid

Complete the word pyramid using the clues provided.

Each clue below corresponds to a level of the pyramid, which indicates the length of the word. Each level of the pyramid uses the same letters as the level above but with one letter added on each row. The letters can be rearranged in each row.

1. **Assist**. As in, "Trump refuses to *assist* low-income immigrants."

2. **Invade**. As in, "the US plans to *invade* Iraq for their oil because 'It's not stealing, it's reimbursing ourselves.' "

3. **Swift**. As in, "the *swift* moral decline of the presidency."

4. **Nappy**. As in, "if only changing government was as easy as changing a *nappy*."

5. **Hopelessness**. As in, "Trump inspires a sense of *hopelessness*."

6. **Utopia**. As in, "*utopia* is now considered to be a world without Trump."

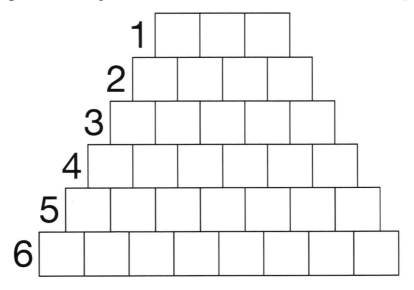

"What you're seeing and what you're reading is not what's happening."

Trick Question

How many people can you count in this artist's
impression of Trump's inauguration day crowd?

"You are witnessing the single greatest WITCH HUNT in American political history – led by some very bad and conflicted people."

Witch Hunt

"It's a witch hunt!" Trump cries, 5 or 10 or 100 times. How is he to convince the nasty, pitchfork-carrying baddies that his friends are not witches. They are not thieves or sorcerers. The cannot be put to trial and burned alive!

Four of Trump's bestest friends have been caught stealing gold. Poor Cunter, Hates, Shohen and Womanafort – however are they going to lie themselves out of this one?

Using the information below, can you figure out what date each man was caught and with how much gold?

- The dates of capture were the 3rd, the 5th, the 10th and the 11th of August.
- The number of gold coins stolen by each person was either 27, 36, 46 or 50 coins.
- Cunter was caught after the person who stole 36 gold pieces.
- The person with the most gold was caught first.
- Womanafort was caught before Hates, and had more gold.
- The person caught last had the least gold.
- Womanafort has less gold than Shohen.
- Hates was caught before Cunter.

*"Women.......Grab them by the
pussy. You can do anything."*

Weird Wording

Can you re-express each of these Trump expressions?

For example: 'A great quantity of currency'
can be re-expressed as 'a lot of money'.

Imitation Bulletin.

Constitutional Exactitude.

"Our country is in serious trouble. We don't have victories anymore. We used to have victories, but we don't have them. When was the last time anybody saw us beating, let's say China, in a trade deal? I beat China all the time. All the time."

ReWritteN

Have fun completing Trump's
most famous expression.

"I think Viagra is wonderful if you need it, if you have medical issues, if you've had surgery. I've just never needed it. Frankly, I wouldn't mind if there were an anti-Viagra, something with the opposite effect. I'm not bragging. I'm just lucky. I don't need it."

RebuS RiddLe

Can you identify the phrase, regularly used
by Trump, that is clued by the following?

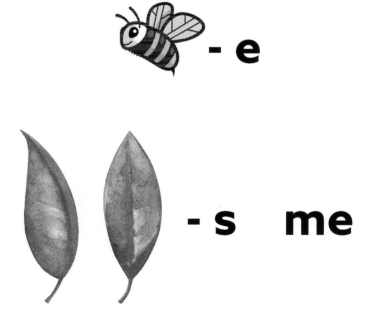

"To be blunt, people would vote for me. They just would. Why? Maybe because I'm so good looking."

Making Sense of Trump

Trump's words are such a pleasure to read, it would be a gross injustice if one were to misunderstand them.

Decode this Trump quote by cracking the Caesar cipher. Shift each letter a consistent amount forwards or backwards through the alphabet. For example, you might replace A with C, B with D and so on until you replace Y with A and Z with B.

PM OPSSHYF JSPUAVU JHU'A ZHAPZMF OLY OBZIHUK DOHA THRLZ OLY AOPUR ZOL JHU ZHAPZMF HTLYPJH?

"The concept of global warming was created by and for the Chinese in order to make U.S. manufacturing non-competitive."

Colour by Numbers

1 – Orange; 2 – Light Orange;
3 – Dark Orange

Solutions

5.
"I could stand in the middle of **Fifth Avenue** and **shoot** somebody and I wouldn't lose **voters**."

7.
Namibia

South Africa

Chad

Botswana

Somalia

13.
Laugh up One's Sleeve

15.
Joe Biden

Barack Obama

Kim Jong-un

Vladimir Putin

17.
Loser

Stupid

Zero

Rude

Unfair

Clown

19.
All of the above

21.

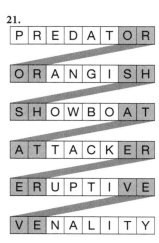

23.

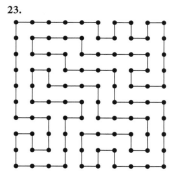

25.
"I'VE SAID IF IVANKA WEREN'T MY DAUGHTER, PERHAPS I'D BE DATING HER."

Solutions

27.

29.
Bad Ombres (how Trump pronounces 'bad hombres')

Winning Again

31.
BAD

DABS

BASED

BIASED

DISABLE

DEBASING

33.
China's emissions are 28% and the country will cap coal consumption. USA's emissions are 15% and the country has left the Paris Agreement. India's emissions are 6% and the country is fighting air pollution. Russia's emissions are 5% and they support the Paris Agreement.

35.
SENSE: NONSENSE and SENSELESS

MAY: DISMAY and MAYHEM

SHIT: BULLSHIT and SHITTING

BURDEN: OVERBURDEN and BURDENSOME

37.
Out of Control

39.
Our choice of solution is:

Hold my **covfefe**

Ivanka Trump is **complicit** in Trump's agenda

Two Corinthians were walking down the road

We must do **cyber** better

This is a **yuge** win

It's not false, it is simply **alternative facts**

Be sure to find a **council** to deal with your legal matters

41.

64

SOLUTIONS

43.
"I'M THE LEAST RACIST PERSON YOU HAVE EVER INTERVIEWED."

45.

```
V V E O O V O V E C E E E F V
F F E C C F V O E E E O C F V
F E O C F E V E F O F F V F O
C E F F E V O O E E F O V C C
E V O E E E C F E F C O C E E
C F E O F V O F E F E E E O E
O O C C F E E F E F E F F F O
E V E V V V E F F E E E E F C
O F F O E F E F E O C F F E F
F E O F C C E V V E O O V C F
V V O O O E E F E F F C C O F
E F O V E O E F E V F V F V C
O O F F F E F C F F F C E O O
E V F O V E E F E E F V F V F
F V V E C C E C F E F V E O E
```

47.
AID

RAID

RAPID

DIAPER

DESPAIR

PARADISE

49.
Clearly there are 1.5 million people

51.
Shohen was caught on August 3rd with 50 gold pieces. Womanafort was caught on August 5th with 46 gold pieces. Hates was caught on August 10th with 36 gold pieces. Cunter was caught on August 11th with 27 gold pieces.

53.
Fake News

Political Correctness

55.
Believe Me

57.
"IF HILLARY CLINTON CAN'T SATISFY HER HUSBAND WHAT MAKES HER THINK SHE CAN SATISFY AMERICA."

IMage Credits

Printed in Great Britain
by Amazon